Quain

Other Offences

ANN DRYSDALE

Independent Innovative International

Published by Cinnamon Press
Meirion House, Glan yr afon, Tanygrisiau
Blaenau Ffestiniog, Gwynedd, LL41 3SU
www.cinnamonpress.com

The right of Ann Drysdale to be identified as author of this work has been asserted by her in accordance with the Copyright, Designs and Patent Act, 1988. Copyright © 2009 Ann Drysdale.
ISBN: 978-1-905614-84-4
British Library Cataloguing in Publication Data. A CIP record for this book can be obtained from the British Library.

Designed and typeset in Palatino by Cinnamon Press. Cover design by Mike Fortune-Wood from original artwork: Beryl Cook © 2000 taken from The Bumper Edition, Victor Gollancz, London. Reproduced by permission of Rogers, Coleridge & White, London.
Printed by Y Lolfa, Talybont, Ceredigion.

Acknowledgements

The Red Mud of Lydney, Old Boats and *Sleeping Together* were first published in *Discussing Wittgenstein* (Cinnamon Press, 2009); *The Bingo Bus, St. Woolos Cathedral* and *To Camelot* were first published in *Real Newport* (Seren, 2006)
Thanks are also due to the editors of the following publications in which other poems have appeared: *Acumen, Equinox, The French Literary Review, The London Magazine, The Chimaera, The Flea* and *The Shit Creek Review.*

Contents

In November 1859 the critic John Ruskin wrote to
Dante Gabriel Rossetti that his sister Christina's
poems...

...are full of beauty and power. But no publisher – I am
deeply grieved to know this – would take them, so full are
they of quaintness and other offences.

Oh, dear.

For Harry
An unexpected blessing in a lucky life

First-footing

Sun on the snow. We are first up, first out
To lay our claim to the unprinted page.
I trudge great boots along the lower margin.
Dog scribes his private joy across the slope
In wild graffiti, praising his own nature,
Writing as the ox ploughs, the ancient way,
Turning the footprints like Etruscan script
Now right, now left, in his innocent progress.

We lie at last in animal communion
Looking down at our own handiwork—
Manipulated whiteness, bearing witness
To two fools' early-morning fortitude.

Look. Bottom left hand corner. Something stirs.
A squirt of multicoloured bobble-hats.
Children, coming about their own business.
Lids of recycling boxes, plastic bags
Lugged up the field, trundled across our writing
And ridden down and down and down again
Obliterating all our evidence.

A universalising metaphor...
Don't even think about it. Home. Soup. Crossword.

Punk and Poetess

...for punk and poesie agree so pat
you cannot well be this and not be that...
Robert Gould *1660-1708*

Alas, poor Robert; Orpheus you weren't
But still you got your plucking fingers burnt.
You badmouthed Sappho for her 'guilt and gout'
And so the Sisters ripped your daylights out.
Poor soul, you were, to borrow from The Bard,
Hoist, willy-nilly, by your own petard—
Not lifted high by pyrotechnic art
But skittled by an ill-considered fart.
Prometheus you weren't, but from afar
You shed a little light on what we are.

A Postcard from Roscoff

This is for you. To celebrate the sharing
Of everything we had the other night;
The joy of loving and the ache of caring,
Laughter and lust, devotion and delight.
Your having trusted me to share a place
Where memory put magic into things.
Seagulls and surfboards with their mirrored grace
Testing the possibilities of wings.
The tantrums of the storm outside the window
Both blessed and spiced the peace we took to bed
But what did Eve conceal beneath the pillow
Where Adam laid his all-too-human head?
Only a little gift of honest fruit—
Care without cant and love without pursuit.

Thirteen Syllables of Safety

Georges Albert Eduardo Brutus Gilles de la Tourette:
I wear the words around my neck like an amulet
That I can touch when I am tempted to disobey
The secret imperatives, as I have done today.
Their sound unifies certainty and coincidence
So that when duty is overruled by circumstance
And I do not perform my devotions properly,
Giving in to the inhibition of company,
Rejecting my script in favour of euphemism,
I say the names quietly, like a catechism
That can save me no matter how far from grace I fall.
This is the last ritual, the one that pays for all.
This spoken, all manner of thing shall be well with me.
But if unuttered, Venice will sink into the sea.

A Cat in the Garden

Amid the torn upholstery of dead birds
Old Tom goes carefully about his work.
Digging in overstated pantomime
He plants his small, soft, aromatic turds.
These, in his wisdom, he is sure will feed
Attenuated turf and wilting weed
Till, in the fullness of slow-funnelled time
A jungle will arise to serve his need
Wherein things small and succulent may lurk
To satisfy his gentlemanly greed.
It will obliterate the simpering sun
And make a dark Valhalla for his soul
When time takes its inevitable toll
And all nine linnet-lunching lives are done.

The Bigger Picture

9th April 2003

You saw it on TV—the footage showed
The mighty Ozymandian overthrow,
The falling statue and the cheering crowd—
And probably believed that it was so.
But see the picture taken from above
In black and white, a single grainy still
Which irresistibly reminds one of
The early work of Cecil B De Mille.
The close-up cheering of a small élite
Was caught on careful cameras, but not
The roadblocks at the end of every street
Lest uninvited extras spoiled the shot
Of History being created there
In one small corner of an empty square.

Danse Macabre

On the 4.45 from Paddington

The leg encroaches on the central aisle
With no concession to the circumstances.
It hogs the spotlight centre-stage awhile
And, unacknowledged by its owner, dances.
The metatarsus spreads to take the strain
As the man pushes but, in spite of him,
A rogue electric spasm in the brain
Sends tremor after tremor through the limb.
With sudden understanding I can see
Through the good trousers to the living sinews
Driven by this insistent mystery.
The train progresses and the dance continues:
Behold the last gasp of ill-fated man—
Jiggered, he jigs his leg because he can.

Definite Article Reduction

A pleasing piece of the vernacular;
Grudging acceptance of an obligation
To pay respect to the particular
When passing on a piece of information.
A nod to a grammatical necessity.
A furtive tongue-tap just behind the teeth;
A subtle sign of specificity
Implying something secret underneath,
Suggestive of a certain sacrosanctity.
A badge of difference, a mark of pride.
A claim to regional identity,
Acknowledgement of a north-south divide.
A shibboleth. A statement. All of these,
Yet bugger all to do wi' t'price o' peas.

The Only Criteria is...

A knee-jerk reaction to the reading of one of my own press releases, wherein I had explained how I chose the poems for a particular project.

Oh, I'm frightfully cross with Amanda;
Her syntax is sadly inferior.
I sent her the thing with 'criterion' *(sing.)*
And she altered the word to 'criteria'.

Oh, I'm fearfully miffed at Amanda—
The point of my piece is diluted;
I had meant to convey in a scholarly way
That my yardstick was closely computed,

That I only considered one question,
That only one test was applied,
That each separate voice was a straightforward choice,
That I set other factors aside.

Oh, I'm sorely dischuffed with Amanda;
I'm as peeved as a pedant can be.
I abhor the misuse; the linguistic abuse
Which the world might attribute to me.

So, learn from my sorrow, Amanda
And two hundred times write it down—
A singular verb has a voice of its own
And it calls for a singular noun.

Glosa

Aspiration might become
a pre-owned Mercedes
do not roll or squeeze
but pick up your own tab.
> from Jump Start *by Tony Lopez:* Devolution *(2000)*

Once inspiration was a necessary
First step towards eventual success.
Next came adventures in vocabulary
And then experiments with sound and stress.
The special mouthfeel of the crafted object,
The absolute conviction in your head
That this was what you felt about the subject
And this the only way it could be said.
With skilled investment of the mounting sum,
Who knew what aspiration might become?

Now —*funding makes you aspirational*—
So fabricate what generates the ready
And if that means the ugly and irrational
Then go for those, and never mind the heady
Pleasure of making something worth repeating
And knowing what it is you're aiming for.
You can achieve it without ever meeting
Any of the sad old criteria.
Settle for second-best, whose accolade is
A bit of skirt in a pre-owned Mercedes

Define the middle ground and aim below it;
The spirit of the age will show you how.
The past is not the province of the poet;
Poetry should be of the here and now.
Latinate diction is a gross offence.
Verse should not rhyme unless by accident
Nor should it scan, nor, God forbid, make sense.
The reader must determine what you meant.
Seize, then, the zeitgeist by the balls, but please
Have some decorum. Do not roll or squeeze.

Found poems are a labour-saving caper
(Best to ignore the fact that someone lost them)
A painless, mindless way of filling paper.
Old boundaries collapse after you've crossed them.
The laundry list, the memo, the prescription;
It's written—rip it off and put it in!
The condom packet and the job description...
Art is a buffet lunch—sod discipline;
Love bids you welcome. Blunder through and grab
What turns you on. But pick up your own tab.

Trying Again

It's all a bit of an act of faith.
Stepping out into the old arena
With threadbare kit, and not entirely sure
If it will still work under field conditions.

And oh, it does! The cunty, clitty bits
Are still a go. They still remember, bless 'em,
How human bodies operate *à deux*,

Loving has many faces. For so long
She has been wearing only one of them
And feels at home in it. Then, suddenly
Faced with exquisite possibility
She feels a reflux of the old, first fear.

Recycled virgin, clinging to the last
To her prosaic knickers. Giving in
After a decent interval. Feeling
Old questions posed by unexpected hands;
Finding she knows the answers.

                      But alas,
She has forgotten the peripherals!
The quick leap of the heart at the sight of him
After short absences. The unasked questions.
And all that internal debate about
The telephone. To call or not to call…

'Chef is particularly good at puddings'

—or so it said on the menu…

They chose two different desserts and traded
Spoonfuls of self-indulgence, then succumbed
To one last sweetness. *Waiter—the wine list—*
Muscat de Beaumes de Venise?   Not by the glass, Sir.

He ordered a half bottle—*What the hell!—*
A taste, a smile, a nod, *We'll keep the cork…*
Before they left he pocketed the bottle.
As he boarded his train he gave it to her.

Back in the digs, facing a night alone
She helped herself to the last of the wine.
Took a quick swig straight from the sticky neck,
Savoured the long, slow, solitary finish
Filling her mouth, feeling his honeyed absence
Languidly marinating her redundant tongue.

Dialogue

He might be coming tonight, said Heart to Head.
No he won't, Head replied, firmly. You heard what he said.
I know, said Heart, but still he didn't exactly
turn me down flat.
Well, he wouldn't, would he? said Head,
you know him better than that;
what he said was 'barring a miracle' —
I thought you understood.
Granted, he did, said Heart, but he also said
he would if he could.
If he'd meant to come, said Head, he'd have mentioned trains;
he'd have confirmed the time.
So he forgot, so what? said Heart.
Since when has that been a crime?
Go on, said Head, firmly but gently. Pick up the phone,
ring and un-book the hotel.
Not yet, said Heart. But I will.
Why do you carry on playing, said Head
when there's so little chance of winning?
Poor Head—am I 'doing you in'? said Heart, grinning.
Death, even by a thousand cuts, said Head,
is still, ultimately, Death.
'Hope springs eternal in the human breast',
said Heart, under its breath.
That was unworthy of you, said Head,
it's a cliché, and it's ugly.
'L'espoir luit comme un brin de paille dans l'étable',
said Heart, smugly.
Straw doesn't shine in stables, said Head,
it just lies there, soaking up shit.
That's right, said Heart. That's it.
Face it, said Head, not unkindly; he isn't coming tonight.
I know, said Heart. But he might.

Confessio Amantis

Last night I came to stay with you and saw
She'd put her number on your freezer door
In multicoloured magnets, clearly done
So you could see it from the telephone,
And, underneath, a green capital X,
With overtones of ownership and sex.
Just for a moment it unhinged my heart
—*You're not getting away with that, you tart!*

It took a furtive finger-flick, no more,
To axe that X and drop it on the floor.
I didn't pick it up, you would have seen,
I let it lie there, futile, fat and green.
At first I felt triumphant. Then I knew
I couldn't do a thing like that to you.
Lying awake beside you in the night
I rose and went downstairs and put it right.
I undid my deletion, and instead
Added another kiss. Lower case. Orange.

Not Much News...

How nice of you to ring. So unexpected.
No. I'm not busy. Yes, I'm on my own.
I wasn't doing anything important.
Just happened to be sitting by the phone.
You don't have to apologise. As always
You got the benefit of any doubt.
I didn't feel neglected in the slightest,
I just assumed you'd rung while I was out.
Odd that you should have caught me at this moment,
First time in ages that I've thought of you.
Oh, blue-arsed fly, love, if you get my meaning,
It's been a very busy week or two.
I've read a lot of proofs for other people.
I've drafted several chapters of the book.
It didn't register you hadn't written;
I haven't hovered long enough to look.
I've caught up with a load of correspondence
And over half of it has been to you.
I tore it up and told myself I'd sent it
Because that's what unhappy people do.
Gave myself toothache biting on a bullet.
Was not much taken with the taste of lead
So spat it out and wrapped it in a hanky.
Opted for doing something else instead.
Decided to apply the skills God gave me
To doing something that I do quite well;
Made an asbestos jacket for a snowball
So as to give it half a chance in hell...

Let's do Lunch…

Oh, where is it heading and where will it end?
Liaison of lovers or food with a friend?
I answered *yes, please* but my heart said *no, thanks*
As I suddenly saw myself swelling the ranks
Of the ladies who lunch with their Afternoon Men
Again and again and again and again
With *rillettes* of rabbit, or *moules marinière*
As the only connection between any pair.

Lunch isn't dinner, which ends up in bed;
We part on a pavement with everything said.
He'll ring me up later but won't talk for long
And I feel in my water it's all going wrong.
There used to be music but not any more
So I know where I am and I've been here before,
A little bit tipsy, a little bit high
On the scent of the cheek that I'm kissing goodbye…
Old Spice… Aramis… Eau Sauvage… Vetiver —
First wind of the end of another affair.

Birthday Song

Christina Georgina, I don't give a hoot—
Balls to the bird and the watered shoot!
A pitiful puddle I lie alone in;
Semen, snot and serotonin.

Birthday, Birthday, Boursin and gin
Another fine mess I've landed in

I've slewed it, screwed it, buggered it, blown it
I won't own up to how long I've known it
It's all my fault and it isn't fair
And if I didn't love him then I wouldn't care

Birthday, Birthday, Boursin and gin
Another fine mess I've landed in

From the first sweet yes to the last sad kiss
I suppose I've known it would end like this
He didn't dissemble, he didn't deceive
But I dared to hope and I chose to believe

Birthday, Birthday, Boursin and gin
Another fine mess I've landed in

The beautiful baton is gone, gone, gone
I've run my race and I've handed it on
And I'm telling myself it's a lucky escape
But I'm hoping she trips on her way to the tape

Birthday, Birthday, Boursin and gin
Another fine mess I've landed in

My head's full of cheese and I'm pissed as a rat
And I don't give a fuck what you think about that
My scansion's shot and my language foul
So I'll stick my fingers in my ears and howl—

Birthday, Birthday, Boursin and gin
Another fine mess I've landed in

Hindsight

I wish I hadn't built a double bed.
I acted on a knee-jerk need to please.
I put the wrong spin on the things you said.

A gesture to embrace what lay ahead —
A sort of act of faith, like Ulysses.
I wish I hadn't built a double bed.

I made a cradle for your sleeping head
Just as he did for his Penelope's.
I put too much weight on the things you said.

I worked like billy-o. Look where it led —
A waste of effort, energy and trees.
I wish I hadn't built a double bed.

Still, now at least I know where fancy's bred;
How wishful thinking fosters fantasies.
I put too much faith in the things you said.

I'll use the wood for something else instead.
Bookshelves, perhaps, or storage for CDs;
I didn't really need a double bed.
I'll find a place to keep the things you said.

Dust

It undulates in angles, moved by the draught
That fingers its way unbidden under lintels,
Coagulates in corners, forming swathes
Lent substance by random gatherings of fur.
Over time I have become accustomed to it,
Overlook it mostly; aware of it only
In the uncomfortable presence of others.
It is familiar. It grows. It changes.
Each time the front door opens
It scuttles across the room in confusion.
An old friend not quite, as the phrase goes, with us,
Whose soft hands quiver in a fluttery welcome,
Wild eyebrows asking, aghast, *who are you, who are you?*

The Rights of Spiders

For John Mole

And what should I do in Illyria?
My brother he is in Elysium.

Spare me the martyrdom of card and cup,
The act mistakenly perceived as kind.
The awful, arbitrary scooping-up—
Arachnid out of sight and out of mind.
Often an upstairs window is involved;
No time to spin a lifeline as we fall.
Okay. It's relocated. Problem solved,
Means home and safety gone beyond recall.
We are not dirty or malevolent
We're not destructive and we do not smell.
For merely being inconvenient
We are cast out into a hopeless hell.
Insiders outside might as well be dead.
Ah! better mangled be than banishèd…

Glenys dances

For Glenys Dowdswell,
who told me her secret

My friend Glenys is fond of dogs
She quite likes cats and she's fine with frogs

But the sight of a spider is enough to propel her
From a standing start to a mad tarantella

No fight, no flight, no choice of chances
Show her a spider and Glenys dances

With a tick-tock timestep the pace is set
Then a kick and a flick and a quick pirouette

She's a thin bone bobbin wound round with wire
Her face is frozen and her feet on fire

With a tip-toe tapping to a tum-titty-tum
Like a skilled paradiddle on a military drum

Her fierce flamenco flattens the floor
As she inches by flinches to the distant door

Where she forces her resources to a *grand jeté*
And the last-gasp chance of a clean getaway

Chanson de l'Homard, Thibault

I am the boon companion of Monsieur de Nerval.
I am privy to his secrets and those of the ocean.
I do not bark.

I am mysterious, bereft and sad.
When I walk with him in the cool of the Palais Royal
we cut a fine figure, outmincing one another.

When he raises his hand to tip his hat to a lady
I am hoisted aloft at the end of my mythical ribbon
and I beat time with my lovely castanets,
my thin legs swimming in air.

Accident Watchers

I am waiting alone for the X15
At the bus stop on the old road through town
While on the bypass, thirty yards away
Behind a low brick wall, an accident
Has happened. The police are there.
And the fire service. And the accident watchers,
Leaning on their elbows along the wall.

I hope nobody died; that there's no blood
To feed their ghastly expectations,
No unfortunate exposure of the helpless
To the scrutiny of the muttering ghouls.

A car stops in the place reserved for buses,
Parks awkwardly. Two people scramble out.
Big guy with an earring, woman following.
Catches me staring at him, looks defensive.
Well, you gotta be nosey, haven't you?

No, I say. *No, you haven't. You've got choices.*
He switches off his face, guiding his girl
Towards the gawping wall, where a man stoops
To hoist a child up for a better view.

Roadside Shrine

Somebody's daughter died here. She was ten.
The school bus swerved and crashed into the railings.
Several were hurt. They mended most of them.
One was too badly broken and she died.

Real people loved her. Miss her every day
In some way or another. Feel angry
Because of her broken promise. Feel sad
Because she isn't with them anymore.

But who are those who added to the pile
Of tawdry, ill-considered artefacts
Before the whole thing slid into neglect?
Strangers perhaps. Probably meaning well.

Eschewing nature's gentle rites of passage
They instigated a horrific withering
With ersatz flowers, simulated dew
Adhering to cloth petals. Glue-drop tears.
A debased currency for buying into
The *oooh!* and *aaah!* of someone else's loss.

The largest tribute was a new pink bear
Tied in an attitude of crucifixion
To the railings at the place the bus hit.
It suffered eloquent disintegration.

The eyes went first. Then for a while it stared
With two pale patches at the constant traffic
Till merciful emissions rendered it
Dull grey all over. It began to smell.

Slowly its shape shifted. Relentless rain
Got sopped-up into the innards of it;
Its belly sagged like a seventh pregnancy
Until the seam gave and the wet guts spilled.

They got the driver for it. Made him pay.
The kids ganged up on him. 'Too fast' they said,
With solemn wide-eyed hindsight. 'Too swervy'.
But perhaps they were driven irresponsibly
By adults who should have known better.

Dear Heart…

I'd like a word with you, my inner poem;
Have you time? I know what it is you're doing
Now I have seen for myself the breakdown
Of your new independent prosody,
The red ink dwelling on the random stresses
Of your undisciplined running rhythm.

We have outgrown the iamb, you and I;
I, having lately come into my strength
Am stimulated by experiment
Nevertheless, it's hard to see my own
Meticulously orchestrated epic
Dissolving into syncopated prose.

What do you have in mind for the coda?
Is it the quick kick and the sudden silence
Of a brisk Audenesque buggering-off
Or will it have a touch of comedy,
Me bowing out to fibrillating giggles
As you die laughing?

Acid Trip

Willow bark, willow bite
First drug I've done tonight
Wish I may, wish I might
Muddle through another night

Ye tiny clots, cumulative contusions
That block the pathways and create confusions
Become as dust dispersing in a river
My willow wand shall banish thee forever.

Strip the willow, set it going
Hold the rhythm, keep it flowing
Ease the valves that stop and start
The secret chambers of my heart

Sing a song of sunshine
Boozy bottoms up
Five and seventy milligrams
Swirling in a cup
When the stuff is swallowed
The traffic starts to flow
And all the little corpuscles
Go marching in a row!

Acid trip, acid trip
Take another little nip
Wish I may, wish I might
Wish again tomorrow night.

Changeling

He stretches out his hand across the desk.
About the size, he says, *of the first joint*
of my little finger. I look, carefully.
It isn't that much larger than my own.

One unstressed syllable of a dactyl.
The end of ignorance; a piece of poetry.
Surely too small to be malevolent?
Just inconvenient and untoward.

Real living tissue, single-mindedly
Bent on continuing its own existence
Looking to me for nourishment and safety
Which it is in my power to deny.

He offers me a moment to decide,
Which I decline. I do not have a choice.
I shall abort you, little afterthought,
But not without a ripple of regret.

I wanted to have a picture of you;
I tried to buy one on the day they found you
But I was told the deal did not apply
To neoplasms—*only to babies*.

The Red Mud of Lydney

On a field trip to Gloucestershire, not long before he died,
The tired leaves of autumn were committing suicide
To the threnody of drizzle which was clearly in cahoots
With the red mud of Lydney that was sucking at my boots.

We were following our colleagues to the villa on the hill
With Philip in the wheelchair, doing splendidly until
We heard a noise behind us such as speedy people make
And turned and saw a four-by-four that wished to overtake.

The cure for our predicament was well within his gift;
His flat bed trailer might have offered us a lift,
But he gave the horn an irritated toot as if to say
That he was heading up the hill and we were in the way.

The man in the Land Rover didn't try to pass,
He made me lug the wheelchair through the lateral morass.
He watched me as I struggled but he wouldn't meet my eye,
Just raised his own to heaven with a hissy little sigh.

It took me every ounce of strength to haul it off the track
And I knew as I was doing it I'd never haul it back.
He found a gear and roared away and left us helpless there.
Oh, I would've pulled my forelock if I'd had a hand to spare.

Each time I see the wheelchair standing empty in the shed
Still muddily encrusted in that special shade of red
It galls me and appals and transports me back again
To the loneliness and hopelessness of Lydney in the rain.

Old Boats

There is no water in the old harbour;
The *Sea View* is a snare and a delusion.
A few old boats lie drunken and decayed
Behind the sandbar that denies them life.
This whole adventure has been a disaster:
All you had wanted was to see the sea.

I lay down by your side in the stale room
Trying to come to terms with disappointment.
Although I know I teetered into sleep
Weeping for you and me and the old boats,
I dreamed for them the return of the sea
Feeling it for them, happy in the dark.

And, Oh, the touch of it! The merry lick,
The cheeky elbowing of their underneaths
And then the bold shouldering-up of them
From the sucky clutches of the dreary mud.
Now balancing, careful at first, and then
The great tipsy surge of the communal rocking
Their timbers singing along to the tinkling of halyards
And all yelling together — *Thalassa! Thalassa!*

Sleeping Together

'To sleep with' has become a euphemism
For fucking, humping, shagging, or whatever
Leads to orgasm, to the spurt of jism
That signals 'tools down' for the jobbing lover.
Sleeping with someone is an act of love—
Another phrase that raises nudge and wink
When it is innocently spoken of—
Though not erotic as the dullards think.
Sleeping is quiet time for private study;
A heaven-given opportunity
Of cherishing another human body
In all its perilous proximity,
Its promontories and its recesses,
The busy music of its processes.

Faking it: For Matthew Arnold, in Dover

You seem so sad tonight
And I have listened carefully, sighing
Along with you in all the right places.
I love you, though I wish you didn't feel
The need to dignify your own tristesse
With classical allusion. Never mind,
What is this 'being true to one another'
Unless it has to do with keeping faith
With one another's vision?

Alas, how we dissemble. Oh, my love
There is no tide in the Aegean. Sophocles
Would never have surprised his shingle naked.
If he was torn to pieces by the dogs
Of existential angst, they were set on him
By some other metaphor. The sea of Greece
Springs no surprises. Nor indeed does this.
The hush and shush echoes the dying fall
Of lovers' music. I will play it for you.

Come from the window; no more talk of darkness.
I will comfort your long withdrawing sigh
And hold you for a while. I will be true
To everything that you have said tonight.
There will be time enough for what I know.

How the Emperor Shun paid for his Cucumber

He told me of the Emperor Shun, the mystic flier
Whose astral self went to the market to buy a cucumber
Which he found in his hand when he later awoke in bed.
Somehow I avoided the obvious; I asked merely
What he had used to pay for it. We both laughed.

That's what I miss most. Flashed grins of shared silliness;
An eye to catch in company. A hand to hold.

When someone thoughtlessly threw out his ancient raincoat
I wept for it, howled for it, hopeless in the knowing
That I would never fall into the arms of it again,
Calling on God and Jesus, my Mum and whoever;
But only the Emperor Shun stepped forward to help.

He said, *Go for it*. I was appalled. No Emperor
Should ever descend to meaningless vernacular.
But he finally sold me the notion of astral travel
And I held his hand and leapt out into the dark.

We flew to a charity shop in a faraway city
Where I found the coat on a rack. I knew it at once.
Five-ninety-nine. But I stole it. Reclaimed it, rather,
Having spent too many tears on it already.
I clutched it, rolled in a bundle, to my breast;
Found it so later when I awoke in bed.

Now night after night I play my game with the Emperor.
Together we go for the raincoat and bring it home.
Alone, I slip into it like a precious dressing-gown
Rolling it round myself, overlapping and holding,
Sniffing lost wrists in the cuffs of the great crossed sleeves.
My fingers fumble the fuzzy past in its pockets
Till I fall asleep in the Marks-and-Spencer hug of it,
Quite safe, and not sad in the slightest any more.

Monstrance or Reliquary

When the Emperor is re-stocking his wardrobe, he usually shops in Paris.
Raymond Tallis: *Not Saussure*

January, and her first time in Paris.
She has looked forward to it all her life,
saving her schoolgirl French for forty years,
knowing that one day fate would bring her here.

Musée de Cluny. She is fascinated
by a small lead box with misted windows
and the label: 'Monstrance or Reliquary'.
One and the same thing to a bit of bone
from a long dead saint. Show it and keep it;
serve and preserve it. But it bothers her.

A window on the Boulevard St Michel,
Sale! Reduced! Everything must go!

Red satin underwear. Exquisite packaging
for a model of bodily perfection
albeit polystyrene. Bum a plum
just short of ripe. Perfect for making jam.
She is disturbed by having thought of that.

Exquisite tits; pert pears on scarlet saucers
offered to view, held up for admiration.
Monstrance indeed. Her own breasts would be better
held in check by a stricter discipline;
adorned by hindsight and imagination.

The little knickers! Not a brazen thong;
a pert frill, rather—a slight draught would flutter it
like a bird in a bush. But not her style.
She could imagine checking manually
If she had actually got them on.

Monstrance or reliquary. Not the same.
Well, to a saint, maybe; not to a sinner.

Dishcloths of Heaven

Tutor: *Help yourselves to scrap paper from the box.*
No need to read what's on the other side...

Why did I question the implied instruction
With all its echoes of Examination?
I was consumed by the desire to know
What Bluebeard kept in the forbidden room.

So that's what happens to them, all those entries
To all those competitions. Like a fool
I had presumed that they would be destroyed.
Shredded, perhaps. Incinerated, even.

And now I know that this is not the case;
I have looked back, like Orpheus. Picked the apple.
Turned round and stood to watch Gomorrah burn.
Here is a poem by a boy called Ben.

A lost poem; a found piece of paper.
One of a thousand-odd. An aspiration.
The rules will have said 'non-returnable'
And mentioned the discretion of the judges.

There is a sort of silence in the room;
The makey-learny poets writing hard,
Doing exactly as they were instructed,
Taking no notice of the other side.

While I provide the sound of furtive searching
Fishing around in my bag for a pencil—
2B, 3B—softer than that—six, even—
Aware that I am writing on a dream.

The Defeated Hare Questions
the Value of Retromingency

Trick question: what can the hare do that the tortoise can't?
Smart answer: urinate backwards

It blinks as it slinks bandy-leggedly into the spotlight
To the roar of the crowd and the laurels and the champagne
And yes, you can guess at the cause of the celebration:
Hey, no shit, Sherlock—the tortoise has done it again.

I am flat on my face on the ferny floor of the forest.
I've been snivelling, dribbling and muttering into the moss
And wiping my eyes with my ears (and it can't do that, either)
And telling myself that I don't give a twopenny toss.

I ought to be used to it, given how often it happens;
It's the way of the world and I don't have the right to complain
But it hurts and I'm sad and I wish it were me on the rostrum.
I'm alone in the dark and the tortoise has done it again.

Omniscient Pan, who distributed gifts to your minions,
Why on earth did you give me a retrodirectional cunt?
For what is the point of the power of pissing behind me
When the tortoise is always, always, always in front?

Sudden Gold

We can do it; we know that we can find
A new way of living, a heaven of a kind…
Here we come, looking for gold.
        Song: Blaina Boys, 1930– *Huw Williams*

Money from Europe has transformed the High Street.
The furniture is a baroque delight;
Matt black enamel has been finished off
With liberal embellishments of gold.

They have not sprayed the paint but laid it on
Carefully, by hand, with proper brushes.
A Blaina boy, bare-armed and beautiful
Puts the last touches to the last lamp post.
Bagoas, dancing his love for Alexander
In the court of the Persian king. He hovers
On the balls of his feet, bending, reaching,
Touching. Teasing the shoulder of the pillar
With little kisses from his goldtipped fingers.

My face is stretched with grinning.
This is my own gold, mined in distant places,
Traded-for on the road to Samarkand,
Hoarded against hard times. Now I am spending it;
A moment of erotic celebration
Before the inevitable palimpsest.
Soon it will all be overwritten with
Felt-tipped inanities—*Leanne woz ya*—
And spurts of dogpiss, dribbled down the plinths,
Will dry to fossil flowers in the sun.

Fag Hag

A song for an unsung relationship

One of my students, now my treasured friend.
Beloved Graduate. I cherish what you gave me.
Not virgin sex, but a far harder coming;
First public utterance of the big word gay.

I cherish who you are; our strange relationship,
Your cheeky challenges — *Play chess or shag?*
If we're still on our own five years from now,
We'll get married, is it?
Ringing me rather drunk on Christmas Day:
It's three o'clock. I thought you'd like to have
A personal message from your own queen…

This is to celebrate the day in Paris
When we awoke together side by side
In our square twin beds and separately
Availed ourselves of the stark white shower,
Its shelves littered with shared cosmetic secrets.
I emerged decorously dressing-gowned
To find you fully dressed before the mirror,
Using your hairbrush to arrange your beard.

Don't look like that, you said, discomfited,
I do this, otherwise it looks a mess.
But I stood shocked at how near I had come
To planting the suspicion of a kiss
On the back of your neck.

Bugger this for a Game of Soldiers

The story has it that when the computer wizards fabricated the battle scenes for Lord of the Rings, the Director decreed that each figure should be programmed to act as an individual and, during the first conflict, some of them ran away...

Hiding in the enhanced hills of the antipodes
We are doing not too badly, all things considered.
We have each of us chosen to step outside the picture
And watch it dispassionately, without benefit of popcorn.

We happy few, we voluntary out-takes—
Virtually indestructible, having no substance—
Sought out our several ways into this haven.
Like Legionnaires, we do not discuss our reasons.

We are a small fistful of hand-knitted fictions,
With fellowship programmed digitally into our pixels;
Having been created utterly true to ourselves
We cannot now be false to one another.

And so we fadge, we Orcs, Elves, Wraiths and Rohirrim,
Carousing round the fire in a ring.

Christmas Day in Rothéneuf

St. Malo played dead with its eyes tight shut,
Lying low under loud siege from a sea
Whose sullen picket had been stirred to militance
By a force ten *agent provocateur*.

Mad English. We walked the Emerald Coast
In time to our own music; suck and plop
Of sensible footwear, underlining
The rhythmic rough breathing of the Gore-Tex.

And in Rothéneuf, the *patisserie*. Open.
Not just for bread with its cold overtones
Of transubstantiation. Alongside
Lay a display of tempting specialities.
They had risen early to greet the Christchild
With the best that a baker had to offer,
Their selling of such indulgences pardoned
By the wicked permissiveness of birthdays.
We bought likewise; one of these, one of those,
Some of all of it, almonds, sugar, cream…

We took our treasure down to the wild beach,
Seeking a place away from the storm's bravado.
Under an upturned boat, huddled like monkeys,
We had a party for the Birthday Boy
And while we licked delight from sticky fingers,
Thin flakes of pastry, winnowed by the wind
Went merrily to heaven—the angels' share.

Return of the Native

The big hen went broody again in spring,
Sat on her collection of china eggs and golf balls
Till I treated her to a box of shop-bought chicks.

While she was busy rearing her whistling treasure
Her sisters and daughters made the most of summer,
Hoeing happily under the shrubs in the garden
Cheerfully sharing their accidental findings.

Today I brought them back, the old broody
And her growing pullets, thinking how pleased they'd be
To be home, how gladly the others would welcome them,
How they would croon tall summer tales together.

It was war. A messy, mindless confrontation,
No beak-holds barred. A loud inhuman confusion.
The adolescents hated their little sisters,
Dibbled sharp scissors into their baby feathers,
Making them squeak and duck, making them kowtow.
The maiden aunts begrudged their sister's triumph
And tried to drive her off; she in her turn
Turned on her elder daughters, shrieking and sweeping
Down in the manner of a high-prowed warship.
Returning native, rewriting the old rules,
Strutting and striking-out in defence of them
Against fierce sallies of collective resentment.
Pulled feathers drifted over bloody chaos.

The violence was too much. I chickened out.
Hustled the whole lot early into the ark,
Eclipsed the evening sun with a tarpaulin
And told myself that by tomorrow morning
They will have made a start to sort things out.

They will find their own ways to get along
Just as they always do. But something's broken now
Past all but a botched repair. Summer is over.

Notebook

On 18th July 2004, Christopher North told me that Ted Hughes took a notebook with him to every momentous event at Moortown, because if he didn't write it down as it happened, he would forget.

Oh, no, you didn't, did you? Please tell me
There was no notebook. There wasn't, was there?
At least, not all the time. Not in the small hours
When the ewe strained in vain and the lamb died
Or later, when the calf lay in the grass
After the struggle. Did it just happen, then?
And were you divorced from it, taking notes?

You owed them all; they needed both your hands
And your whole brain. Commitment. Concentration.
The next thought jolted like a cattle-prod;
That little falling-in. The sick suspicion
That you were never there. Not in the real way
Of stockmen. Doubting your authenticity
Because of what I know, not out of books.

I know it needs two hands to lamb a ewe.
I know that books are useless in the rain,
Nothing will make a mark, the pages stick.
You would have stood apart, then, sheltering
The precious notebook from the elements,
Your big self from the grubby goings-on.

And if that's true, none of the rest is true.
You took the notes, but did you pull the trigger?
You told the pain but did you feel the grief?
Tell me there was no notebook. If there was,
Then you were only a poet all along
And I am only a farmer.

The Glitch in the Carpet

The quick hurt in the heart at the sight of the typo
When it's too late to do anything about it.
The hollow moment when the second thought
Owns up to having been a bad idea.
Recurrences of self-recrimination
Kick, like hiccups, at the sore ribs of the head.

To this pain is applied as palliative
The well-meant, ill-considered observation:
'It's said that to produce a perfect carpet
Is sacrilege; *Allah* alone is perfect'.

The humility to spoil something precious
Purposely on a point of principle
Is arguably hair-shirt holy, but
To dedicate incompetence to the Lord
In the Damascus-dazzle of hindsight
Insults both His intelligence and mine.

Don't Worry about Heaven...

For John Whitworth

...What GOES ON in Heaven, that's what I want to know.
Do they have cricket and Marmite and public libraries?
        John, via email. *8.20am. 8.4.07.*

Oh, will there be cricket in Heaven—
The impact of missile on bat,
The sensation of play
Going on miles away
From the place in the grass where you're sat?

But of course there'll be cricket in Heaven
For isn't it just what God meant;
Making poor flannelled fools
Follow mystical rules
For the promise of tea in a tent?

But will there be Marmite in Heaven?
Will I feel the familiar drouth
As it trammels the tongue
Like an ill-fitting bung
Till it cleaves to the roof of the mouth?

Well, there's bound to be Marmite in Heaven!
Apart from its tasting divine,
They would need brewers' yeast
At the family feast
Or they couldn't change water to wine.

And libraries, are they in Heaven
Addressing the cultural gap?
Do they stand in the streets
Holding volumes like sweets
To enlighten the average chap?

Not libraries, dearest—but bookshops;
You can gaze at their goodies all day
But, just as on earth,
You decide what they're worth
And you browse and you choose and you pay.

To My Last Publisher...

I've been to a marvellous book-launch
With Peter and Patty and Paul
There were nibbles and wine
And the frocks were divine
But no conversation at all.
Oh, Peter was happy to see me;
I could tell by the set of his jaw
But the hosts didn't know me; they looked me right through—
Which most other publishers do tend to do—
So I sat at the back and thought smugly of you.
I couldn't have liked it more!

I've been to a marvellous book-launch
The Waterstone's' sales pitch was grand
And my brownie-points soared as I settled on board
—*on me seat wi' me book in me 'and.*
Dear Peter was plying his Parker
And soon came across when he saw.
I said *Will you sign mine?* and he smiled and said *yes*
But I had to keep stumm for I dared not confess
That I'd ordered it cheap through the dear PBS.
I couldn't have liked it more!

I've been to a marvellous book-launch
The book they were launching was *Food*
And it did seem to sell
And the author read well
And some of the poems were rude.

But the whole thing was frightfully cliquey
With a strange sort of *esprit de corps;*
They gathered in groups, speaking Welsh to their kin
And I felt a bit sad that I couldn't join in
Till I thought about bullfrogs and stifled a grin.
I couldn't have liked it more!

Hoping it might be so…

For Peter Reeves
to follow a reading of Hardy's 'The Oxen'

It was Christmas Eve in the farmhouse
Their bedtime was overdue.
They were kissed and 'night-nighted' and overexcited
And one of them asked *Is it true?*

The kids had discovered the poem
About how the animals kneel
On Christmas Eve. They were keen to believe
And they asked me if it was real

And I hadn't the heart to tell them
It was 'just something out of a book'
So I foolishly said that if they went to bed
I would go out at midnight and look.

I had no real intention of going,
At least, not at that time of night.
I might pop out at ten for a *shufti* and then
I could say I had seen no such sight.

Why should it be asses and oxen?
Why not the dog or the cat?
But the authorised versions of ancient assertions
Are seldom as simple as that.

Now Christmas needed preparing.
I applied myself to the task.
I'd decide what to say on the following day.
I hoped they'd forget to ask.

The goose was asleep in the oven.
The gas was on number three.
It was starting to smell so to check all was well
I went out to the kitchen to see.

The goose's rich juices were oozing
Overflowing the edge of the tin
They dripped from the door but did not hit the floor
For a volunteer had stepped in.

The dog lay under the cooker
Twitching his whiskery lips
With his long tongue flicking, religiously licking
The oleaginous drips.

I wrapped up the children's presents
Wishing there could've been more.
Forgetting the fable, I tidied the table
And lovingly laid it for four.

The dog staggered in from the kitchen
And settled himself at my feet.
As I fondled his ears, he confirmed my ideas
Of what makes a Christmas complete.

Then he heaved and threw up on the carpet—
A puddle of grease from the roast,
So I leapt to my feet—and it sopped up a treat
In the *Yorkshire Evening Post.*

Soon all the unspeakable gubbins
Was as clean as the Queen could desire
And I rolled it all in a decorous ball
To chuck on the back of the fire.

*(Pause for audience to appreciate the significance of this—
Oh, no, you didn't? —Oh yes I did!)*

The bundle of newsprint and goose-fat
Went off like a mighty grenade
And sprinkled with sooty and gritty confetti
The preparations I'd made.

I had to rewrap all the presents.
I had to scrub down all the chairs.
It was almost next morning when, drooping and yawning,
I started to stagger upstairs.

But a promise is a still promise
So before I fell into my bed
I did the long tramp with the paraffin lamp
Down to the animals' shed.

I lifted the latch on the 'stable'
And there in the lamplight I saw—
The animals lying, all snoring and sighing,
Asleep in the golden straw.

Two goats and an elderly wether
And a heavily pregnant cow.
It was just as I thought; I should have to report
They were none of them kneeling now.

But the sense of my presence engendered
A frenetic activity burst;
They were caught by surprise and attempted to rise
In the usual way—hind legs first.

Then they saw it was me in the doorway
So they froze for a moment there
In puzzlement, with their forelegs bent
And their haunches up in the air.

So I said to them softly *Sorry*
And closed the door on the scene.
And I thought about kings and shepherds and things
And how it might have been.

And I told the kids in the morning
Because I thought they should know
That some things must just be taken on trust,
Hoping they might be so.

Jo-Jo's Mother

I'm very glad you came the woman said
From over by the window. I could see
The monkey in her arms was crisp and dead.
She turned and smiled and held it out to me.
Take Jo-Jo for me, would you please, young man?
Just hold him carefully and he won't bite.
Tell him a little story if you can.
He's being very difficult tonight.
She handed me the sorry piece of fur;
The little twiggy arms were bent and stiff.
I said *Hi, Jo-Jo* and I smiled at her
But she was staring hard at me, as if
She knew she'd seen me somewhere, couldn't quite
Remember where it was our paths had crossed
And then she gasped and rushed at me in fright,
Took Jo-Jo back and stood there, looking lost.

The Bingo Bus

The ladies of Winchestown are going south for the 'Ousey.
Flashing their passes, they accrue on the sideways seats
At the front of the trundling bus as it growls down the valley.

The twitter is constant; a narrow, high range, like bats,
Unmoderated in its content, for who can overhear them
Other than dogs and peculiarly sharp-eared children?

They all chew gum. In their youth it was thought unseemly
So they chew very fast to make up for so much lost time,
Redeploying the involuntary motions of old mouths.

They take on their gum like ballast before boarding.
They work it as they talk, quick-flicking it like the shuttles
Of the flannel weavers in days even they don't remember.

Tongues toss the soft pellets like small boys in blankets;
Teeth, false and furious, catch them and roll them ready
For another somersault as the tongues move in again.

And so it goes—*allez-oop!*—*à bas!* —*encore!*
A non-stop pantomime of death and resurrection
All the way down to the 'Stute in Abertillery.

St. Woolos Cathedral, Newport

The John Piper Window

Haphazardly conceived and ill-defended,
Against the odds it stands among the dead.
Made and unmade and carelessly extended,
An artless shippon with a lean-to shed.
Each little death has seen it rise again;
A monument one cannot but applaud,
As much to the pigheadedness of men
As to the greater glory of the Lord.
A later spate of damage-limitation,
Replacing broken tiles and rotten wood,
Included a mad act of exultation
Among the shoring-up and making-good
And through a round hole in its dreary skin
A beam of glory alleluias in.

To Camelot

Yobs untie the cabin cruiser
Left to rot beside the river,
Drag her down and turn her over,
Push her out onto the water
    Just to see if she will float.
Big boots crushing frosty sedges
All along the water's edges,
Hurling missiles from the bridges
    At the dented, dying boat.

First she proudly breasts the current,
Rides the river, heir apparent
To the beauty of the torrent,
Off to face her final moment
    Elemental and alone.
But the yobs continue throwing,
Conscious of their power, knowing
They can still control her going—
    One more curse and one more stone!

Laughing with the joy of wrecking;
Shattered screen and splintered decking.
Listing, lurching, bobbing, jinking,
Now she founders, now she's sinking—
    Yeah! Titanic! Gissa shot!
Little bits of broken mirror
Catch the sunset on the river
Where the song goes on forever
    All the way to Camelot.

Beavers

It was a nightmare that I used to have
Before I went to sleep. A fear at kiss-goodnight,
At big-girl-now going upstairs alone;
A what-if, growing as I enumerated
Each brown linoleum stair, into a conviction
So that I slid into a cold bed knowing
That now they were beavers.

Knowing was enough. I did not need to catch them
In the act of changing. That would have been unseemly;
A spying, prying, punishable how-dare-you,
An unanswerable who-do-you-think-you-are.
As far as I know, they never knew that I knew.

There was no disadvantage in being uncertain
As to the nature of beavers. Needing a word,
I picked it thoughtlessly out of the chattering air
Because it frightened me. Beaver was beast extremely,
Alien and other; gross teeth and horrid tails
Like the spilled stuff that issues inside-out
From the hind ends of things that have been run over.
They were mean-spirited, despite their gentle fur;
They laughed a lot, beavers, behind closed doors.

Instinct told me that having sussed their secret
Put me in danger; if it were found out
Unspeakable horrors would clatter down around me
Because of my rash unpicking of the fabric of things.
I pretended sometimes being caught and punished,
Savouring the slow spiral into despair.

Somewhere along the line I grew out of it.
Left it behind. All but forgot about it.
But I have come across it again on the way back
And I am not much helped by my knowing
That it will all probably end as it began.
I am afraid again. Afraid of going downstairs
Into a soft, terminal bewilderment
Presided over by white-coated beavers.

Port of Call

I'll bet that's Olga's daughter said the nurse
To the auxiliary as I went by.
Ooh, she's the spit of her came the reply.

This is a thing I have come to expect
Since I negotiate the same waters
And carry the insignia of our line.

These visits are strange things for both of us:
She never really liked what I became;
I am appalled by what she has become.

Daily I sail along the corridor
Riding the central current, overtaking
The halting progress of the prepossessed,

Hailing the beached craft on their tiny islands,
Greeting the busy bumboats that attend them
Until I reach the wharf where she is moored.

I lie alongside for a little while
Watching the rocking of her fragile timbers
Then slow astern, about, and on my way.

I am the steward of my ship. My duties
Include a full test of the escape drill
Which must be random and without warning.

So it cannot be left till the last day,
When it would merely be inevitable—
Which then, of course, rules out the day before…

And so it goes. I am responsible,
Aware of all the hazards up ahead,
Relying on an untested procedure.

Backwards it comes, then. Nearer and nearer—
Do it, my heart says, artfully, craftily.
Do it. Do it now.

Blue Juice

Familiar name for Sodium Pentobarbital,
drug of choice for veterinary euthanasia...

Ultimate catflap, petdoor into eternity
And all the other merry euphemisms
That blur the hard edge of an act of love.
Blue Juice; tincture of courage and compassion
A rite of passage and a consummation
Of life which has simmered down to essences.

Blackberries, bleeding into the soft palms of children
Who snatch and swap and stuff their greedy mouths
With the free sweetness of the countryside,
Returning home with innocence belied
By the stigmata of their self-indulgence.

Bilberries. Rough wind on the high moors.
Pulling each other down among the wires
Out of its blusterous reach. Helping ourselves
To the rare opportunity of each other
Despite the splatterbruises of the berries
Printing their small betrayals on our skin.

Indelible pencil, drawing illicit pictures
On a licked forearm, making blue tattoos
That shimmer in the spit.

Atropa Belladonna, gentle purple,
Offering itself to me in the garden.
The light is going and I am alone.
I am aware of all the old wisdom,
The *do not touch the tree* imperatives
But finger and thumb reach out instinctively
To take the dare, to pick the fruit, to eat,
To stain my lips with the forbidden juice
Until I dance like Mark Antony's soldiers,
Cannot distinguish truth and fantasy,
Lose my already ineffective voice
And fly till flying takes my breath away.

I had forgotten rain

Waking to overheard conspiracy
Among the ivy leaves. Nothing malevolent
Just the excited whispering of children—
Shush, shush, hee-hee—Oh, wait till she see this…

Gastropods swollen and alive with juice,
Purposeful, moving in time-lapse gallops
As my attention flickers.

The sense of something, a bedraggled shadow
Which disappears as soon as I address it
With the first word that comes into my mouth;
Sorry, I tell it. Sorry, sorry, sorry—
I was elsewhere and did not realise
I had forgotten rain.

I am becoming my grandmother...

Sooner or later, in the great scheme of things,
Women are ambushed by their transformation
Into their own mothers. Mirrors tell them,
Or echoes of some little tetchiness
That still itches under skin that has thinned
To let it out again.

Not I;
I have skipped a generation and will soon
Become my grandmother. It has begun.
No longer can I pass a crying child
Without wiping its nose on my pinny
Or any dog without extending my hand.

I find all kinds of treasures in the street
And take them home with me in a string bag.
I touch flowers, move snails out of the way
Of passing traffic. All these things I do
Regardless of the present company.

The transformation has not gone unnoticed;
Somebody left a hurt newt in a bowl
Outside my door, assuming I could help it.

And now at last I am the world's Aunt Jessie;
Old, fat and ugly, but—hurrah! God loves me!
Daily I hit the road in shapeless lace-ups
Dap-slapping my way across East Anglia,
Now and then turning my face up to heaven
Like a tanned leather bottle full of questions
To diagnose the illness of the wind
And look for little ways to make it better.

Said Yeats's Bones to Hardy's Heart...

Said Yeats's bones to Hardy's heart
What matter where we lie?
There'll always be posterity
And horsemen riding by.

Said Hardy's heart to Yeats's bones
I'm not disputing that
But you are threatened by a truss
As I am by a cat.

Ah yes, the truss, the bones replied
They say it shows them surely
That I am not myself at all
But someone else entirely.

Said Hardy's heart, the story goes
They hunted high and low
But what was in the biscuit tin
The world will never know.

However, on the principle
We two are of a mind—
Muffle the drum and let them come—
To hell with what they find.

They need a place of pilgrimage,
They come in droves to look
And while they're in the neighbourhood
Perhaps they'll buy a book.

We are where we have always been
And shall be through the ages;
We pressed the flowers of our selves
Between our gathered pages

And those who there seek Tom and Will
Won't care where you or I go—
For I am not in Stinsford Church
And you are not in Sligo.

Cliché

1.45 am 25.12.06

The air is soft and still. The dogs' toenails
Click on the tarmac. Their warm faeces
Swing from my finger in a plastic bag.
Christmas Eve has morphed into Christmas day
Without the intervention of a night.

There is no darkness. Lights along the bypass
Cast their thin shadows over the verges.
Electric greetings hanging in festoons
Urge happiness and merriment, including
The odd oblique reference to the Christ.

And now the bird, the old poetic constant,
Treacles his little heart over the pudding
As if to blackmail me into responding;
He seems to think he's Keats's nightingale
Or Shelley's skylark. He's been done to death.

Tom Hardy got the bugger bang to rights
And poor Mad Jack, God rest him, had a go
So what on earth can one more poet do?
Another poem? Might as well. These tears
Are unbecoming in the elderly.

Water

For Kenneth Steven, who wanted a sonnet

Its small manifestations move me most.
The jewelled trickle on a chilly bottle.
The snotty gobbets of dissolving frost
on nostril-whiskers of outwintered cattle.
The cold sheen covering a limewashed wall
where the upwardly mobile damp has gathered.
The diamante shimmer over all
the webs with which the windowframes are feathered.
Bright drops tossed from the wet necks of cormorants
who have begun to come too far upriver
in search of what the sea no longer grants,
questioning our perception of forever.
I write my name in it, careful and clear,
to watch it dull, dry up and disappear.

The Last Lamp

I am the last lamp at the end of the street;
A lightheaded pole with a pool at my feet.
I can't relocate even though I might like to;
I'm something substantial to padlock your bike to.
I'm ballsy and feisty and bubbly and bright
And I wear a brave face through the long winter night;
A bold boulevardier, flamboyant flâneur,
A keeper, a peeper, a one-eyed voyeur.
Like a daffodil bulb I come on in the dark,
Becoming the star to each wandering bark;
Yet I limit the vision of all who pass by
For I highlight the pavement by hiding the sky.
To men a convenience, to dogs a urinal,
I'm photogenetic and phallic and final.

Notes

Page 8. 'Punk (ie slut) and Poetess' was a phrase applied to Aphra Behn, adapted from Robert Gould's contemporary crowd-pleasing satire.

Page 15. The Only Criteria is indeed! But alas, what can one expect from a girl whose name is a gerundive of obligation?

Page 16. Glosa: The glosa is a Spanish form introduced by the court poets in the fourteenth century, based on an Arabic pattern that has been traced back to the ninth. It has two parts, which are normally written by different authors. The first part—the *texto* or *cabeza*—consists of a few lines which set the theme for the entire poem. Typically this will be a stanza taken from a well-known poem or poet. The second part—the glosa proper—is a gloss on, or explanation of, the *texto*. It takes the form of an ode, with one stanza for each line of the *texto*. Each stanza in turn expands upon its corresponding line, and ends with a repetition of it. It is arguably, therefore, the earliest form of 'found' poetry.

Page 28. The Rights of Spiders. John Mole, in his book *This is the Blackbird* (Peterloo Poets 2007), has a poem 'Instructions for Catching the Spider' which seemed both reasonable and humane until I discussed it with the spider who has lived for years on my highest bookshelf among the works of Shakespeare.

Page 30. *Chanson de l'Homard, Thibault*. Thibault was the name given by Gerard de Nerval to a lobster he rescued from the nets in La Rochelle. He kept it in Paris for a while and is said to have taken it for walks on a ribbon in the gardens of the Palais Royal. Nobody knows what became of it, but years later Nerval showed Théophile Gautier a grubby bit of string, saying it was the girdle of Madame de Maintenon. When good-humoured doubt was cast on this, he said that it was really the garter of the Queen of Sheba. That night he used it to hang himself from a grating in an alley behind a dosshouse. I have often wondered whether it was really the treasured lead of *petit Thibault*.

Page 35. Acid Trip. The acid involved here is not *Lysergic acid diethylamide* but *Acetylsalicylic acid*. Sorry.

Page 40. Faking it... It is probably unfair to suggest that Arnold's *Dover Beach* might have been inspired by post-coital tristesse, but I'm right about the shingle—I got the facts from a book: *Aegean Sea: Tides minimal, with a range of only about 40cm/15 in. English Channel (Dover): Tides between 5 and 7 metres.*

Page 45. The Defeated Hare... This is one for the TAPITS—the generous people who hand me such serendipitous *trouvailles*, along with the promise 'there's a poem in that'.

Page 56. To My Last Publisher. I showed this poem to Peter Finch who said it was very funny and that he was 'honoured that I'd bothered'. Had he minded, it would not have been considered for publication. Other names are fictitious and the homage to Noel Coward wholly deliberate.

Page 63. The Bingo Bus. 'Stute—the Miners' Institute. Once every South Wales mining town had one.

Page 70-71. Blue Juice. Belladonna is supposed to have been the plant that poisoned the troops of Marcus Antonius during the Parthian wars. Plutarch gives a graphic account of the strange effects that followed its use.

Page 74. Said Yeats's Bones to Hardy's Heart. Some people believe, because of a mysterious truss found among the remains, that a Mr Hollis lies in Yeats's grave—and most people have heard the story of the family cat's having stolen Hardy's freshly-excised heart.